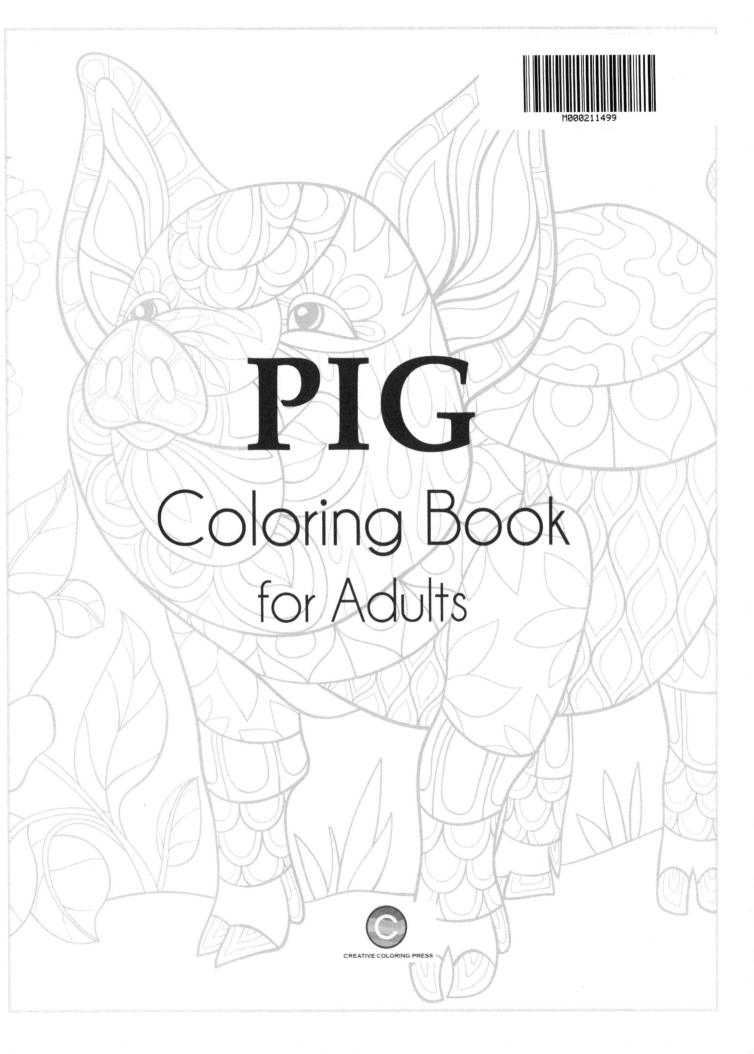

PIG
Coloring Book
for Adults

CREATIVE COLORING PRESS

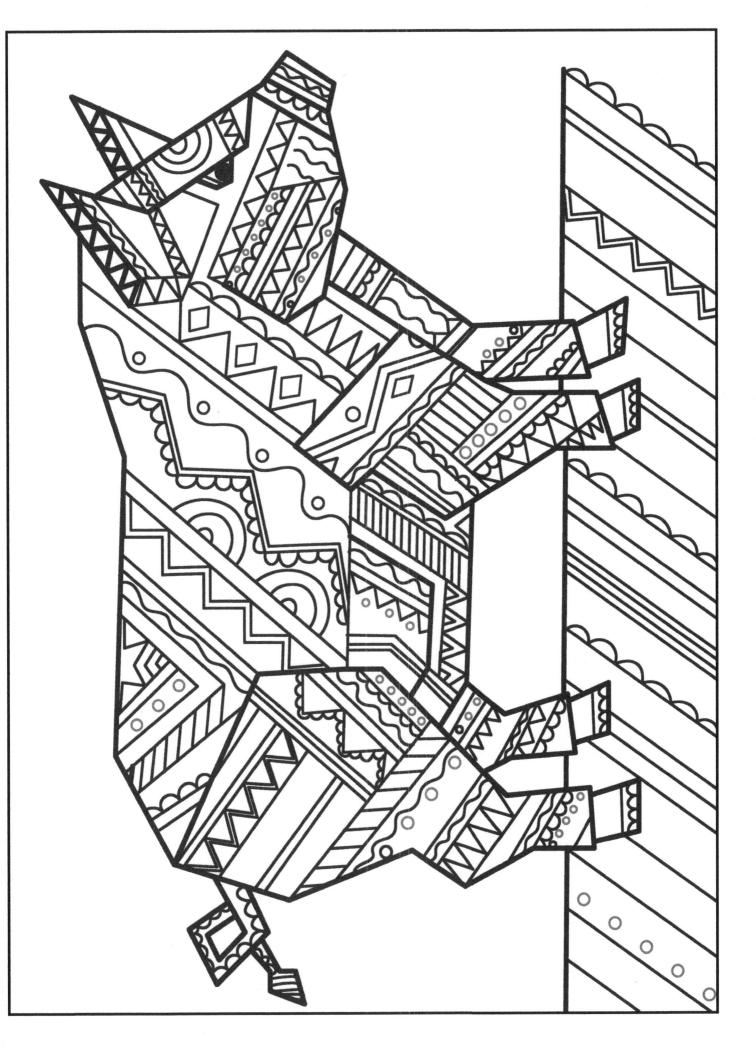

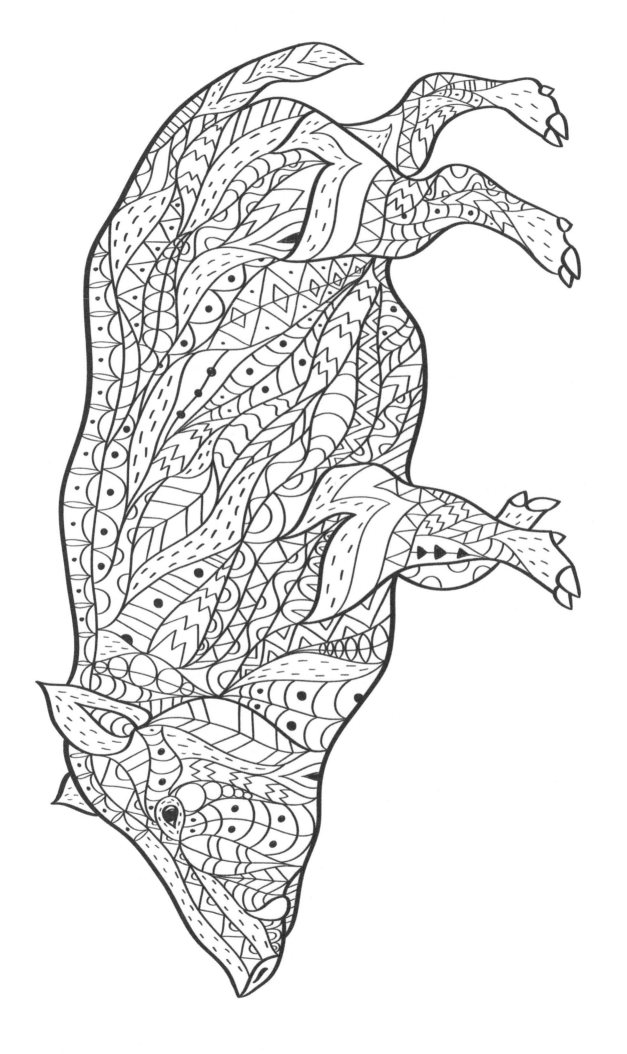

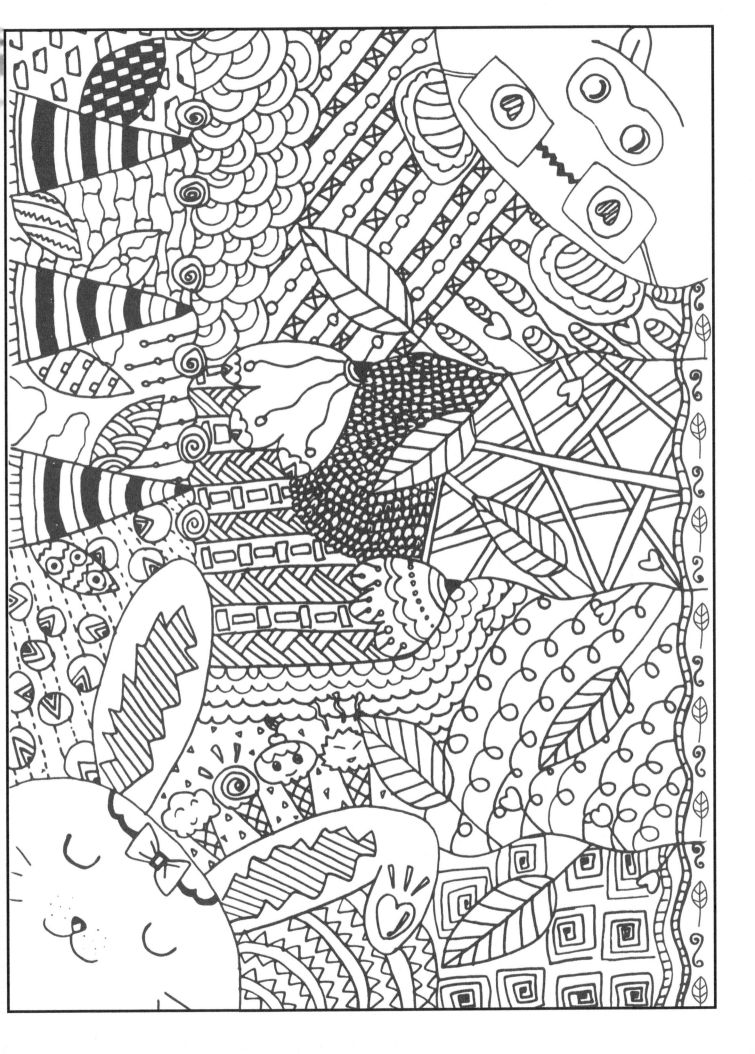

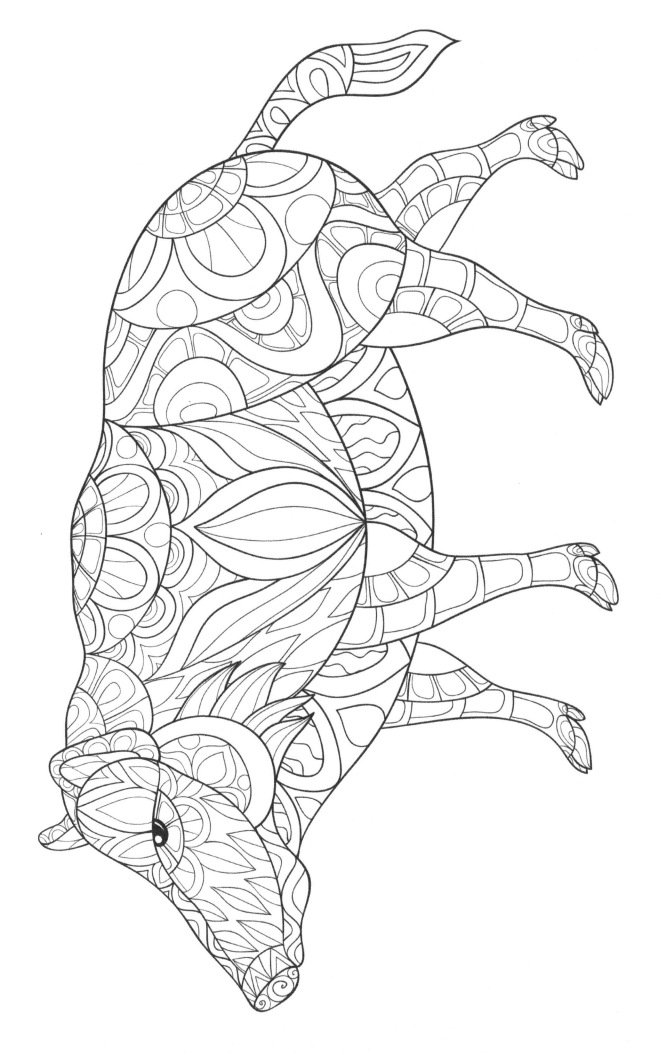

Sign-Up to Get a Free Coloring Book

Subscribe to our newsletter and get a free printable coloring book of some of our most popular illustrations. Plus you'll receive special offers, sneak peeks at new releases, and more. Visit us at www.creativecoloring.co for details.

We hope you've enjoyed this coloring book and that is brings you many hours of fun, stress relief, and creativity. We'd love to see and share your creations.

We want to hear from you!

Send us your ideas, suggestions, and finished artwork:

www.creativecoloring.co
facebook.com/creativecoloringpress
Instagram: @creativecoloringpress
Twitter: @creativecoloringpress

Bonus

Turn the page for bonus pages from some of our most popular coloring books.

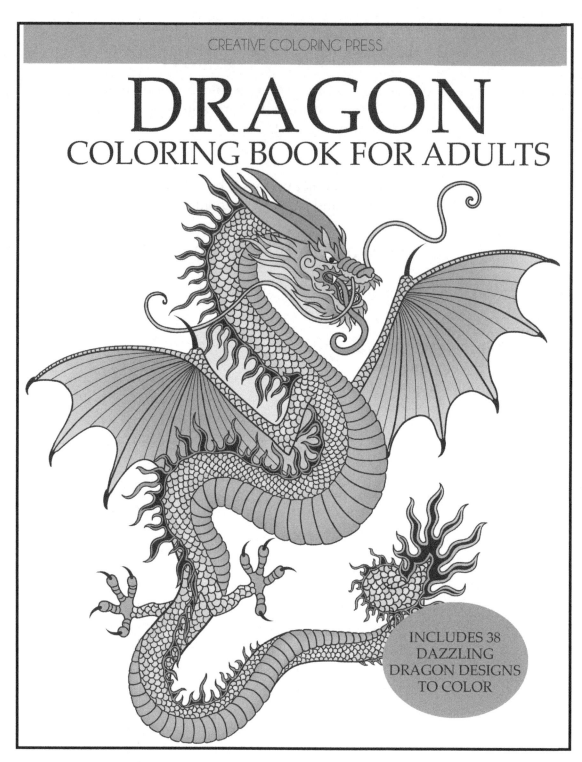

Chickens and Roosters Adult Coloring Book by Creative Coloring Press
Available now at Amazon.com, Barnes and Noble, and other online retailers.

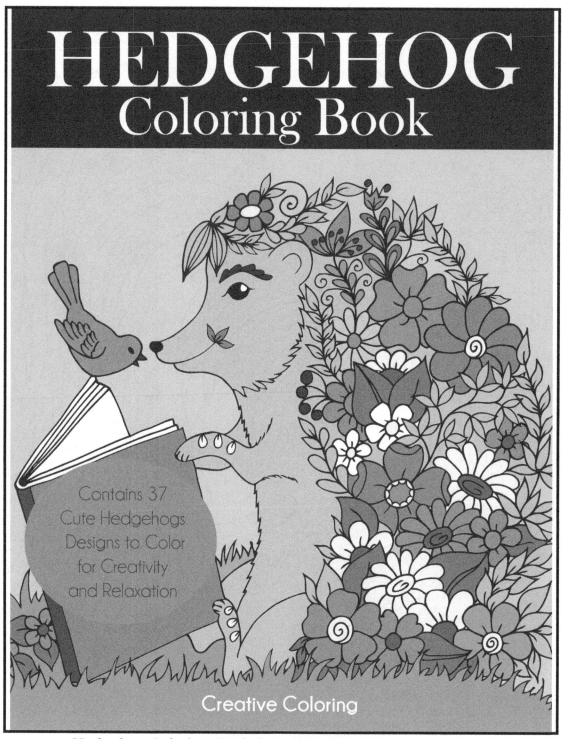

HEDGEHOG
Coloring Book

Contains 37
Cute Hedgehogs
Designs to Color
for Creativity
and Relaxation

Creative Coloring

Hedgehog Coloring Book for Adults by Creative Coloring Press
Available now at Amazon.com, Barnes and Noble, and other online retailers.